*"That which is highly esteemed among men
is detestable in the sight of God."*

Luke 16:15, NASB

DEPENDENCE

UPON THE

LORD

K.P. YOHANNAN

BOOKS

a division of Gospel for Asia

www.gfa.org

Dependence upon the Lord

ISBN: 978-1-59589-015-3

Published by gfa books, a division of Gospel for Asia
1800 Golden Trail Court, Carrollton, TX 75010 USA
phone: (972) 300-7777
fax: (972) 300-7778

Printed in the United States of America

For information about other materials, visit our web site:
www.gfa.org.

11   12   13   14   15   16   17   18 / 10   9   8   7   6   5

Table of Contents

Introduction

> I am the true vine, and My Father is the
> vinedresser. Abide in Me, and I in you.
> As the branch cannot bear fruit of it-
> self, unless it abides in the vine, neither
> can you, unless you abide in Me. I am
> the vine, you are the branches. He who
> abides in Me, and I in him, bears much
> fruit; for without Me you can do noth-
> ing. By this My Father is glorified, that
> you bear much fruit; so you will be My
> disciples (John 15:1, 4–5, 8).

In our walk with the Lord and our service to
Him, we must continue in the reality of this
timeless truth every day—that "as the branch

cannot bear fruit of itself, unless it abides in the vine," neither can we unless we abide in Him. My prayer is that you would grow in your dependence upon the Lord alone and experience the joy of a life lived in full reliance upon Him.

CHAPTER ONE

Are You Qualified?

Remember David and Goliath, that familiar Bible story we were taught in Sunday school? We smile as we remember the flannel board display of this childhood story. Maybe you can even recite how the story unfolds: The young David, with sling and stone in hand, walks up to Goliath, trusting God, and lets loose the shot that caused the huge giant to fall.

But the story of David and Goliath is so much more than flannel board and familiarity. It *truly* happened. It was a real war, with real men defending their own country. David *was* just a boy, never skilled or trained in war, and Goliath really was a fearful giant. Step out of the familiarity and put yourself in David's shoes for a moment. Can you imagine how he must have felt when he spoke to his king about victory, only to have the king laugh in his face at his "youthful courage"? Picture yourself in a battle for the first time, your countrymen watching you as you're armed with a childhood toy. Hear the opposing troops chuckle as you pull out your slingshot and grab a stone from your pocket. Watch as some of your countrymen bow their heads in embarrassment as they see you ready your sling. The moment of truth is at hand. How sweaty your palms must be as they steady the shot. There's no turning back now—this is all or nothing.

The story of David and Goliath is truly amazing! It's a remarkable display not only of God's faithfulness, but also of David's incredible dependence upon the Lord. David had absolutely nothing to rely on—not a weapon, not experience, nothing. The only thing he depended on was the ability, faithfulness and power of God. And that was enough! He killed the giant that day—not because of his strength or his plan, but because he was depending upon God to give him the victory.

God desires to do the same in our lives as well, if we would only trust, lean and rely fully upon Him. Like David, we do not need to have a long list of credentials to qualify us to be used by God—simple dependence upon Him will do. Second Corinthians 4:7 says, "But we have this treasure in earthen vessels, that the excellence of the power may be of God and not of us." The treasure spoken of in this verse is God within us. All the treasures of heaven are ours as a gift, to partake of and share with others but held in simple "earthen vessels"—you and I. The NIV translation calls us "jars of clay." God wants us and the world to know that the treasure, the power and everything good that flows out of our lives come from Him, not from us. The jar of clay cannot produce water in and of itself; it can only be used to pour out what it has been *filled* with. God's treasures flow out of us as we depend upon Him, the source of all good things.

Even though we live in a world today in which people are professionals and specialists, with doctors trained to do only certain types of surgery and Ph.D.s with a lot of knowledge in one specific area, God still looks past credentials, searching above all else for a heart that will depend upon what He can do.

In fact, all throughout Scripture it seems God uses the foolish things of this world to confound the wise. That's exactly what 1 Corinthians 1:27 (KJV) says, "But God hath chosen the foolish things of the world to confound the wise; and God hath chosen the weak things of the world to confound the things which are mighty." Numerous times, God finds an ordinary man or woman whose heart is fully dependent upon Him and works through that person in extraordinary ways, showing His power and might and bringing Him alone the glory and honor.

For example, a couple of years ago at our Bible college in Bangladesh, one man who served as a cook at the college desired to enroll in classes so that he could become a missionary. His heart for the Lord was great, but unfortunately, he did not meet the minimum education needed to be admitted into our Bible college. When the head principal heard about the cook's desire to serve the Lord but that he was unable to attend the college, he told the cook that if he wanted, he may sit in on the Bible classes after he finished his cooking duties.

The cook was thrilled with this idea. So every morning and afternoon, as soon as he finished all his responsibilities in the kitchen, he attended bits and pieces of as many classes as he could to learn as much as possible. Soon the school year was coming to a close, with 18 smart, strong, young men ready to graduate from the Bible college and start their mission work. But the first new church in the area was not planted by one of the graduates. The first church was planted by the cook! And after he planted his first church, he turned it over to one of the graduates and went off to start another!

A classic biblical example of God using an ordinary person is found in the life of Noah. Never having built a boat before, Noah had absolutely zero qualifications to do so. But in Genesis 7:5, we find out why Noah was successful in the ark's construction: "And Noah did according to all that the LORD commanded him." Because Noah completely depended upon the Lord to show him what to do, the ark withstood 40 days of the greatest storm the world has ever known. The boat held up against all the beatings of the storm and finally came to rest, with all its animals safe and sound. The *Titanic* was built by men who knew what they were doing. It was specially designed by experts to be unsinkable. Men bragged about the wonderful ship they had built. Yet on its first voyage ever, it ran into an iceberg and went down in the Atlantic Ocean. Hundreds of men, women and children drowned in the ice-cold sea.

From David to Noah, we see that the only qualification to be used by God is absolute dependence on Him. These men were simple, yielded vessels looking to God alone, never relying upon mere human strength, experience or skill. Because of that, God was able to display His greatness through their lives.

CHAPTER TWO

How the Job Was Done

In 2 Chronicles, we find the story of King Asa, ruler of Judah. Having inherited the throne from his father, King Asa tore down all the idols of foreign gods early in his reign and commanded the people to seek the Lord (see 2 Chronicles 14:2–5). Soon thereafter, an army of a million men and 300 chariots attacked Judah. With only a mere 580,000 men comprising his army, King Asa quickly called everyone before the Lord and prayed, "LORD, there is no one like you to help the powerless against the mighty. Help us, O LORD our God, for we rely on you, and in your name we have come against this vast army. O LORD, you are our God; do not let man prevail against you" (2 Chronicles 14:11, NIV).

The Lord was faithful to deliver that great army into King Asa's hands—because he looked to and depended upon Him. The Lord also granted his nation 20 years of peace after that battle.

But oftentimes, the way we start out is not always the way we finish. And this is the reason why I seek to remind us that dependence upon the Lord is an absolute necessity if our lives are to bear any good fruit. We will never come to a place at which we will no longer need to look to God, depending fully on Him to provide strength, life and power. No matter what comes or goes, this spiritual truth remains central to the work of God in us and through us.

Twenty years after experiencing God's faithfulness, King Asa is faced with another battle. Baasha, the king of Israel, begins to attack Judah by walling in the city, letting no person or supplies in or out. King Asa panics and quickly sends word to the King of Aram, asking him to break treaty by attacking Israel, forcing King Baasha to abandon his attack on Judah to defend his own country. The king of Aram does so, King Baasha flees back home to fight off his new enemy and Judah is kept safe (see 2 Chronicles 16:1–6).

We can just sense King Asa's sigh of relief as his nation is saved from Israel's attack. On the surface, his plan seemed to work; not only was he able to get rid of his enemy, but even gained a new ally in the process. But of this victory the Lord said,

> Because you relied on the king of Aram and not on the LORD your God, the army of the king of Aram has escaped from your hand. Were not the Cushites and Libyans a mighty army with great numbers of chariots and horsemen? Yet when you relied on the LORD, he delivered them into your hand. For the eyes of the LORD range throughout the earth to strengthen those whose hearts are fully committed to him. You have done a foolish thing, and from now on you will be at war (2 Chronicles 16:7–9, NIV).

From this Scripture portion, we see that God is not so much concerned with the end result as He is with *how* something is accomplished. If God were only concerned with the end result, He would have applauded King Asa for being so clever as to call on some distant king and devise such a cunning plan. But God clearly called King Asa's plan foolishness because all of it depended on what man could do.

In essence, for the *end* to honor God, the *means* must honor God. If we are seeking to establish a work that will remain for all eternity, if our lives and what we do are to last the test of time, then the motive and the means must be centered and dependent upon the Lord. What matters most is that God is the leading factor rather than our own strength and ability.

This is because anything that is built on the ability, skill and expertise of men will never bear *lasting* fruit. We, like King Asa, can be deceived by quick results. True, everything may look wonderful in outward appearance—the elegance of buildings, the great number of people, the repertoire and esteem—but God looks past all these things into the heart. He knows whether or not a heart is fully committed to Him, leaning and depending upon Him above all else. He knows who has built the house and has said, "Unless the LORD builds the house, they labor in vain who build it" (Psalm 127:1).

Romans 14:23 (NIV) reminds us, "Everything that does not come from faith is sin." When we depend upon ourselves, we cancel out any reason to have faith and depend on God. So then, whatever is done in our own strength, rather than in dependence upon God, is sin. And Scripture testifies that we can bear good fruit only when we, as the branch, remain dependent upon the life from the Vine. In John 15:4–5 (NIV), Jesus said, "Remain in me, and I will remain in you. No branch can bear fruit by itself; it must remain in the vine. Neither can you bear fruit unless you remain in me. I am the vine; you are the branches. If a man remains in me and I in him, he will bear much fruit; apart from me you can do nothing."

When we stop depending upon the Lord, our lives stop producing good fruit. This is exactly what happened to King Uzziah. Becoming king when he was only 16 years old, King Uzziah ruled in humility and depended on God to guide him and give him wisdom to rule. Second Chronicles 26:4–5 (NIV) says, "[Uzziah] did what was right in the eyes of the LORD. . . . As long as he sought the LORD, God gave him success." King Uzziah was successful because he depended upon the Lord. But sadly, as he became a more "competent" king, growing older and having some experience to fall back on, he no longer trusted or obeyed God. Instead, he did things his own way. Scripture says of him, "But after Uzziah became powerful, his pride led to his downfall. He was unfaithful to the LORD his God . . ." (2 Chronicles 26:16, NIV). His life ended in terrible tragedy; he became a leper.

The same downfall also happened to King Saul. He started out little in his own eyes, trusting the Lord in the beginning of his reign. But soon things changed. He became prideful, self-willed and strong in his own strength, seeing himself as important and competent. He stopped depending upon the Lord, and it cost him his throne and his life.

In the end, we must remember that the most important thing is not *what* was accomplished, but *how* it was accomplished. Were things done relying upon you—your strength and your provision—or were things accomplished by relying upon God? Jeremiah 17:5–6 says, "Cursed is the man who trusts in man and makes flesh his strength, whose heart departs from the LORD. For he shall be like a shrub in the desert, and shall not see when good comes, but shall inhabit the parched places in the wilderness, in a salt land which is not inhabited."

The Lord sets the choice before us to depend upon ourselves or to depend upon Him. The rest of Jeremiah 17 tells us the outcome of the man who, indeed, does rely upon the Lord: "Blessed is the man who trusts in the LORD, and whose hope is the LORD. For he shall be like a tree planted by the waters, which spreads out its roots by the river, and will not fear when heat comes; but its leaf will be green, and will not be anxious in the year of drought, nor will cease from yielding fruit" (Jeremiah 17:7–8). Let us be those people who choose the way of blessing by honoring the Lord with hearts dependent upon Him.

CHAPTER THREE

No Confidence
in the Flesh

Back in the 80s I had the opportunity to visit with Keith Green and the staff of Last Days Ministries. For a long time, I had received their newsletters and was quite impressed, thinking they must have some of the finest graphic designers working with them. However, during my visit I came to discover that the artists designing the Last Days newsletter weren't trained professionals at all! They were just kids from the streets whose lives had been changed by Christ. Having given up the right to run their own life, these men and women simply served at Last Days Ministries the best they could. And because of their surrender and dependence upon what Christ could do through them, they were used to do great things.

Even though I've seen God use untrained men and women countless times, my eyes still search for the professionals. Just yesterday, I was looking at an application of someone who desired to serve with the Gospel for Asia staff. The first thing my eyes went to was the section about the applicant's education and experience, scanning what kind of training and expertise the person had.

I am not saying there is something wrong with utilizing the gifts that God has given people or recognizing certain abilities—not at all. The leadership at GFA prays for God to bring people with specific skills and talents to work within the ministry. That is legitimate and appropriate. For it is God who gives us different skills, all so that we can use them to glorify His name. To one He gives five talents, to another two, and to another one, expecting us to invest them wisely (see Matthew 25). But I have seen time and again that a lack of education never hinders God from using an individual.

Please understand; I am not making light of education, skills or talents. But I do believe that it is only as we surrender our abilities to Him—give up our rights to own and rely on our strengths—that He can use us to accomplish great things for Him. There are biblical examples of this. Just think of Moses. Having been raised in Pharaoh's house, Moses received some of the best leadership training of his day. Certainly God ordained this training for Moses, knowing that he could use this later in his life when leading the children of Israel, right? But such is not the case.

While Moses was in the desert as a criminal and serving as a shepherd (one of the lowliest of jobs in that day), God began to prepare Moses for fruitful service. How did God do this? By unraveling Moses' confidence in himself, bringing him to the place where he even said, "God, I can't do the job." It was then that God was able to use Moses in a mighty way because he had nothing of his own to rely upon anymore—no previous training, no experiences to fall back on—nothing. Just simple dependence upon the Lord.

The same is true with the apostle Paul. He was an incredibly brilliant, well-trained individual. He studied under Gamaliel, a well-known philosopher and theologian, and was perfect in the Law. He was a Pharisee of Pharisees. History tells us that Paul was trained to perfectly debate and defend his faith. In Philippians 3:4 (NIV), Paul says of himself, "If anyone else thinks he has reasons to put confidence in the flesh, I have more . . ." and he goes on to list his professional credentials—the things that, under the law, qualified him for service.

Yet after Paul's Damascus Road experience, God did not send him to the Jews where all these credentials would have seemed to be of great value. If I were God, I would have said, "Finally, I have found someone that I can use to impact the whole Jewish nation! Through his abilities, his knowledge of the Hebrew Scriptures and his power of debate, the Jews will finally come to believe in my Son, Jesus." If I were God, I would have said, "Look at his credentials, his education and his experience! He is definitely the one to do the work among the Jews."

But God didn't do that. Instead, He sent Paul to the Gentiles. That doesn't seem to sound right. Paul could have spoken eloquently with the Jews, confounding them with his wisdom and his ability to decisively argue the facts. He knew all the laws, all the Scriptures, all the history and culture. In order for Paul to reach the Gentiles, he had to lay aside everything he knew so well, leaving him with nothing to fall back on. In his own words, Paul said,

And I, brethren, when I came to you,
did not come with excellence of speech
or of wisdom declaring to you the
testimony of God. And my speech and
my preaching were not with persuasive
words of human wisdom, but in dem-
onstration of the Spirit and of power,
that your faith should not be in the
wisdom of men but in the power of God
(1 Corinthians 2:1, 4–5).

It is not that God only uses amateurs, the
poor, the uneducated and those who lack
ability. It is that God will only use those who
will depend on Him—those who will give
Him the glory for what is done. The real issue
is not how much education we have or do not
have. *The real issue is whether we are dependent
upon God.* God wants to use us all—professionals and amateurs alike. But He is not
going to bless a work that leads anyone to
depend more upon his or her own strength
rather than on the strength of God.

Throughout his ministry, Paul learned
how the "power is from God and not from
us" (2 Corinthians 4:7, NIV) and how "our
adequacy is from God" (2 Corinthians 3:5,
NASB), not from our experience or training.
Even after years of preaching and service to
God, numerous churches planted and incredible fruitfulness of his ministry, Paul still

said, "I know that in me (that is, in my flesh) nothing good dwells" (Romans 7:18). In Philippians 3:3 (NIV), he said, "[We] put no confidence in the flesh." May the Lord give us the attitude and understanding that Paul had in this—that we, in our flesh, are incapable of bearing good fruit that remains. But *through* Him, our lives can bear good fruit and bring glory to God.

CHAPTER FOUR

Knowing Him

As the disciples testified of Jesus after His resurrection and ascension, incredible miracles took place. All throughout the book of Acts, we read of how thousands believed on the Lord Jesus, lame people walked and the blind received their sight. As the educated theologians and experts in the Law watched the disciples and the miracles that happened through them, they wondered at their abilities. It says in Acts 4:13 that "when they saw the boldness of Peter and John, and perceived that they were uneducated and untrained men, they marveled. And they realized that they had been with Jesus." True, compared to the theologians of their day, the disciples were uneducated men. These experts in the Law did have greater knowledge of God, probably more knowledge than all the disciples put together. But knowing *about* someone and personally *knowing* someone are worlds apart.

Please understand. You may know the Bible very well, even hold a Ph.D. in theology, extensively knowing Greek and Hebrew. But even with all this knowledge, you can be spiritually bankrupt if you do not know the Lord Jesus Himself. That which made the difference between the disciples and the theologians was the three and one-half years the disciples spent with Jesus. Even the theologians recognized this, realizing that the disciples "had been with Jesus."

Spending time in the Bible does not necessarily mean you are spending time with the Almighty. In John 5:38–40, Jesus pleads with the religious leaders, saying, "But you do not have His word abiding in you, because whom He sent, Him you do not believe. You search the Scriptures, for in them you think you have eternal life; and these are they which testify of Me. But you are not willing to come to Me that you may have life." Even though these men searched the Scriptures, knowing them inside out, His Word was not abiding in them.

And in all their knowledge *about* God, they missed the most important thing—knowing God.

The reason this is so important is because it's only when we come to know someone that we can trust and depend upon him. An example of this is found in the parable of the talents in Matthew 25:14–29. The man who received the one talent buried his instead of investing it like the others. His reason for doing this? " 'Master,' he said, 'I knew that you are a hard man, harvesting where you have not sown and gathering where you have not scattered seed. So I was afraid and went out and hid your talent in the ground' " (Matthew 25:24–25, NIV).

"I knew you were a hard man . . . " and "I was afraid . . . " The real problem was not that the man buried his talent but that he truly did not know his Master, hence there was no trust. This left the man looking for a way to handle the talent according to his logic. And when relationship is absent, so is dependence.

What are some signs or indications of someone who is not depending upon the Lord? I want to show you a few examples:

🞖 *When a problem arises in your life, do you seek the counsel and advice of friends and the people you know, rather than turning to God first?* When we choose to make anything other than God our refuge and strong tower, we turn our dependence from the presence of God and begin to depend on the counsel of friends. This is a dangerous trap.

🔲 *When your bank account is full, do you just dish out money for anything, whenever it is wanted or needed?* Or do you take the time to pray and seek God, waiting upon Him to speak to you and show you how to handle the resources He has given you? By always looking to Him, even in the good times, we show that our lives are fully dependent upon Him and Him alone.

🔲 *Do you, as a parent, spend more time trying to figure out how to raise your children, what route of discipline is best and so on, rather than spending time in prayer for your children?* Praying for and seeking to live a godly life before your children will make more of an impact upon your household than all the "how-to" books you could read.

🔲 *When you are looking for a new job, do you automatically take the one with the higher pay and best benefit package, rather than spending time in prayer and fasting, seeking the*

Lord's decision in the situation? God's ways are higher than ours, and unless we take the time to seek Him, we can miss out on what He may desire for us. Maybe there is someone He wants you to minister to in that lower-paying job. By waiting on God to hear His voice and His direction, we are saying, "God, I depend upon You. Please show me Your ways." And in that dependence, He is glorified and our lives receive His blessing.

▣ *Do you spend days preparing a message, studying different commentaries and books, rather than spending even half the time on your knees, waiting before God?* When the time to hear from God is replaced with anything else, we essentially are turning our eyes away from God and depending on the information we can find, rather than on the words of life that only He can reveal.

▣ *When you are sick, are your first thoughts, "Where is the aspirin?" or "I must call the doctor!" rather than seeking the Lord to heal you?* When we do this, we basically tell the Lord that He is insufficient and that we cannot depend upon Him to heal us. My brothers and sisters, may this not be so.

Please don't misunderstand the point I am making. Medicine and doctors are not bad at all. The Lord has given them to us and heals people through their work. Seeking the counsel of friends is not bad, for we read in Proverbs 24:6 that "in a multitude of counselors there is safety." "How-to" books are not bad; reading commentaries and searching biblical text are not wrong; good-paying jobs are not from the devil. The whole point is where do our hearts look *first?* To all these things, or to the Living God?

There are hundreds of other ways I could mention of how our lives turn from dependence on the Lord. I pray that you would open your heart to the Lord and allow Him to identify these places in you. By doing so, He will be glorified in your life, and you will walk in His blessing because your heart is fully committed to Him. And the Lord has promised, to this person, He shows Himself strong (see 2 Chronicles 16:9).

Conclusion

Psalm 44:5-8 says, "Through You we will push down our enemies; through Your name we will trample those who rise up against us. For I will not trust in my bow, nor shall my sword save me. But You have saved us from our enemies, and have put to shame those who hated us. In God we boast all day long." "Some trust in chariots and some in horses, but we trust in the name of the LORD our God. They are brought to their knees and fall, but we rise up and stand firm" (Psalm 20:7-8, NIV).

It is God's delight to show His power at

work through our lives. He is calling for each of us to trust in Him, to rely upon Him and to see what He can do through us. When we accept His call and choose to depend upon Him, we are able to stand firm, our feet placed on solid ground. Here are the points we must remember in order to stand firm:

- It is important for us to understand that the Lord rejects a work dependent on any thing or any person other than Himself. God desires that we always look to Him, never relying on our own strengths and abilities or depending on anything apart from Him. Be it our talents, friends, family members, buildings, money, or the resources of other people—none of these should become the source of our trust. God uses these as means to help us in our times of need and to further His Kingdom, but ultimately He is the only one whom we can depend on.

- Our abilities, skills, talents and backgrounds have no relationship to how much God can use us. God is almighty and He can do anything, but He has chosen us to partner with Him. He seeks us as jars of clay—channels for His work. God uses us to do His eternal work based on

one criterion: our willingness to depend
on Him and give Him the glory. The greatest saints are simply the greatest receivers.
Relying upon the Lord, they are nothing
but channels; they know this and give
God all the glory.

▣ The more naturally gifted one is, the more
he or she must go through death to self
and pride in order to be used by God.
Our ego is so deceitful. All the talents and
natural abilities given to any of us were
given by God in the first place. Yet we
so easily take ownership of these things
and attribute them to ourselves. We must
realize that God always seeks to bring
us to the place of death so He can work
through us (see Galatians 2:20). When we
surrender our abilities to God, we become
partners with Him, and He accomplishes
great things through our lives.

▣ It is possible to begin with absolute trust
and dependence upon God and later to
be led astray, thinking we had something
to do with the victories. In the midst of
great blessings, we can be rejected by God
because of our pride. As we saw in Chap-
ter 2, King Saul and King Uzziah both fell
because of this. God can do great things

through us, but we cannot take credit for what is His. Paul did amazing miracles, established churches throughout Asia and led hundreds to Christ, but he also said truthfully of himself, "I know that nothing good lives in me" (Romans 7:18, NIV). We are merely the instruments of God.

⊞ On the outside, something can look very wonderful (like King Asa's victory) but in actuality be very displeasing to God. Nebuchadnezzar built a large and beautiful city, but does it stand today? Where is the Tower of Babel in our history? It is a remembrance only of the sinfulness of good-intentioned flesh. We need to keep in mind that that which is esteemed before men is despised by God. If anything in our life or ministry is to count for eternity, it will come forth from Christ as we are dependent upon Him.

Mother Teresa, the woman who gave her life to help the needy in India, was born into a wealthy Albanian family. When God called her to go to the poor of Calcutta, she was a respected principal at a Catholic school. Yet with joyful persistence she obeyed. Despite the worldwide fame and attention that later came her way, Mother Teresa remained

humble and unimportant in her own eyes.
She walked in the reality of knowing that the
fruit from her life did not come from herself
but was merely a by-product of depending on
God and His working through her. For years
she labored among the diseased and dying,
never having received any formal medical
training. Yet her service impacts thousands
even today. Toward the end of her life she
said, "I am convinced that when I am gone, if
God finds a person more ignorant and useless
than I, He will do greater things through that
person because it will be His doing."[1]

What a lesson for us all to learn! I encourage
you, my brothers and sisters, learn the
strength of God, which is stronger than man;
learn the wisdom of God, which is wiser than
man. "Trust in the LORD with all your heart,
and lean not on your own understanding; in
all your ways acknowledge Him, and He shall
direct your paths" (Proverbs 3:5–6). We began
well by trusting in the Lord. Let us now continue
in His strength and live in His blessings.

Prayer

Dear Lord, please show us parts of our lives, whether big or small, where we have not looked to You, depending on Your grace and strength. Father, we want to please You by living lives that bear good fruit. Help us do that and to know You, and in knowing You, depend on You, giving You the glory for the work done in and through our lives.

Thank You for being God, all-powerful and all-knowing. Thank You for having ways that are higher than ours and for teaching us of those ways. Help us to humble ourselves and depend on You for everything. Be glorified in our lives, O Lord. In Jesus' name, Amen.

If this booklet has been a blessing to you, I would really like to hear from you. You may write to Gospel for Asia, 1800 Golden Trail Court, Carrollton, TX 75010. Or send an email to kp@gfa.org.

Notes

Conclusion

[1] Mother Teresa of Calcutta, *The Joy in Loving: A Guide to Daily Living,* comp. Jaya Chalika and Edward Le Joly (New York, NY: Penguin Group USA, Inc., 2000), p. 414.

No Longer a Slumdog

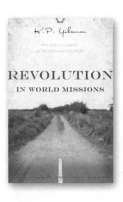

Booklets by K.P. Yohannan

A Life of Balance
Remember learning how to ride a bike? It was all a matter of
balance. The same is true for our lives. Learn how to develop
that balance, which will keep your life and ministry healthy and
honoring God. (80 pages)

Dependence upon the Lord
Don't build in vain. Learn how to daily depend upon the
Lord—whether in the impossible or the possible—and see your
life bear lasting fruit. (48 pages)

Discouragement: Reasons and Answers
Ready to defeat discouragement and move on? It can be done!
Discover the reasons for discouragement, and find hope and
strength for an overcoming life. (56 pages)

Journey with Jesus
Take this invitation to walk the roads of life intimately with
the Lord Jesus. Stand with the disciples and learn from Jesus'
example of love, humility, power and surrender. (56 pages)

Learning to Pray
Whether you realize it or not, your prayers change things. Be
hindered no longer as K.P. Yohannan shares how you can grow
in your daily prayer life. See for yourself how God still does the
impossible through prayer. (64 pages)

Living by Faith, Not by Sight
The promises of God are still true today: *"Anything is possible to
him who believes!"* This balanced teaching will remind you of
the power of God and encourage you to step out in childlike
faith. (56 pages)

Principles in Maintaining a Godly Organization
Remember the "good old days" in your ministry? This booklet
provides a biblical basis for maintaining that vibrancy and
commitment that accompany any new move of God. (48 pages)

Seeing Him
Do you often live just day-to-day, going through the routine of life? We so easily lose sight of Him who is our everything. Through this booklet, let the Lord Jesus restore your heart and eyes to see Him again. (48 pages)

Stay Encouraged
How are you doing? Discouragement can sneak in quickly and subtly, through even the smallest things. Learn how to stay encouraged in every season of life, no matter what the circumstances may be. (56 pages)

That They All May Be One
In this booklet, K.P. Yohannan opens up his heart and shares from past struggles and real-life examples on how to maintain unity with those in our lives. A must read! (56 pages)

The Beauty of Christ through Brokenness
We were made in the image of Christ that we may reflect all that He is to the hurting world around us. Rise above the things that hinder you from doing this, and see how your life can display His beauty, power and love. (72 pages)

The Lord's Work Done in the Lord's Way
Tired? Burned out? Weary? The Lord's work done in His way will never destroy you. Learn what it means to minister unto Him and keep the holy love for Him burning strong even in the midst of intense ministry. A must-read for every believer! (72 pages)

The Way of True Blessing
What does God value most? Find out in this booklet as K.P. Yohannan reveals truths from the life of Abraham, an ordinary man who became the friend of God. (56 pages)

When We Have Failed—What Next?
The best is yet to come. Do you find that hard to believe? If failure has clouded your vision to see God's redemptive power, this booklet is for you. God's ability to work out His best plan for your life remains. Believe it. (88 pages)

Order booklets through:
Gospel for Asia, 1800 Golden Trail Court, Carrollton, TX 75010
Toll free: 1-800-WIN-ASIA
Online: www.gfa.org

CAN YOU DIE

TO YOURSELF FOR ONE YEAR?

School of Discipleship

Invest a year at Gospel for Asia's School of Discipleship and your life will never be the same.

"This was one of the best years of my life."—Matt

You will:

Rescue the hurting and oppressed by working at GFA's home office.

Grow spiritually through challenging classes and personal discipleship.

Intensify your prayer life lifting up the lost souls of Asia.

Travel to the mission field to see firsthand how God is reaching Asia through GFA.

Open to dedicated Christian single adults ages 18-27

For more information, check out the website or email us at school@gfa.org

 gfa.org/school · gfa.ca/school ·  /gfaschool · /gfaschool · disciple365.org